Copyrighted 2019 by. ~~Shumeka ~~

All rights are reserved. Written permission must be secured from the publisher to use44 or reproduce any part of this book, except for brief quotations in critical review or articles.

REFRENCES

KJV SCRITURES

PHYLLIS TARBOX

OBED

BEING FREE PUBLISHING, INC.

ATLANTA, GEORGIA

770-905-2517

LORD DELIVER MY SOUL
"A CRY FOR HELP"

Author

Dr. Shameka Pointer

DEDICATION

I would like to first; GIVE ALL THE GLORY TO THE MOST HIGH for this amazing gift He has blessed me with. I thank GOD for my son named Amari and just his mere presence in my life. He Has seen me at my best but has also seen me at my worst, but we have always made it thru together. For the people who have touched my life in many ways whether good or evil, I'm reminded that ALL THNGS WORK TOGETHER FOR THE GOOD OF THOSE WHO LOVES THE LORD WHO ARE CALLED TO HIS PURPOSE

ROMANS 8:28

For you have delivered my soul from death, my eyes from tears, my feet from stumbling

Psalms 116:8

Introduction

The Soul

What happens when your soul is in turmoil? The soul is the major part of why you do the things you do in your life. Your soul is the core of all your inner issues that flow out of your life. Many are dealing with soul sickness. They are tired, frustrated, angry, confused, and more. Sometimes just living isn't good enough. The pain that is steaming from the soul being sick causes depression, anxiety, and other mental diseases. Just from experience I can truly tell my story of how I knew my soul needed a healing. I would always hear Kelly Price song "I NEED A HEALING FOR MY SOUL", I would always wonder why does she need a healing, but as I got older, I realized hurts, disappointments, and setbacks can be very heartening in which will affect the very soul. When I think about the soul being affected, I get this deep hurt feeling in the pit of my stomach that gives me a sad feeling. The soul is very important when it comes to our everyday lives, but mostly spiritually because one day when God calls us home it has two places to go and that's Heaven or Hell. So, guess what that soul needs to be healed, delivered and set free. I can think of a time when I thought a soul was this evil spirit that comes out of your body. Funny Right!!! But that's what the tv industry constantly shows. As I got to know what it really was it wasn't a soul that came out as a dark figure but also as a light figure which is representing evil and good. So, if I thought that, I'm pretty sure there are others who thought or is thinking the same thing. It's time to educate people on what a soul is and the importance of knowing where it will end up. The soul must take rest one day, so this book is just to inform you, prepare you and warn you to make sure your soul is headed for Heaven and not Hell. Please take your time and read this book. Take a self- evaluation of yourself and make sure if you desire to go to heaven you take heed to the information in this book and release anything that you know is tied to your soul and not of God.

LORD DELIVER MY SOUL

CONTENTS:

CHAPTER 1..........................SOUL TIES

CHAPTER 2............ SOUL TIE SIGNS AND SYMPTOMS

CHAPTER 3........................ SOUL MATES

CHAPTER 4................ PARTS OF A SOUL

CHAPTER 5................... TUG AND PULL

CHAPTER 6...................ENTANGLEMENT

CHAPTER 7.................. IMMATURE SOUL/MATURE SOUL

CHAPTER 8.......................... SOUL FIGHT

CHAPTER 9.......................... DELIVERED

CHAPTER ONE

SOUL TIES

Many may ask the question, what is a soul tie?

Soul Tie is an emotional bond that form an attachment. They may be Godly, or Ungodly, and pure or demonic. Most people use the term soul tie to refer to connections linking people. Soul ties are not necessarily sexual or romantic. But I really want to discuss the Ungodly soul ties. So, I will give you seven signs of Unhealthy Soul Ties.

1. **You are in a physically, emotionally, spiritual abusive relationship, but you feel so attached to the other person that you refuse to cut off the connection and set boundaries with them.**

2. **You have left a relationship (maybe long ago) but you think about the**

other person obsessively and you can't get them off your mind.

3. Whenever you do anything, make a decision, have a conversation with someone, and so on- you feel like this person is with you or watching you.

4. When you have sex with someone hopefully your husband or wife, you can hardly keep yourself from visualizing the person with whom you have a soul tie.

5. You take on negative traits of the person your soul is tied

to and carry their offenses, whether you agree with them.

6.You defend your right to stay in a relationship with the person to whom your soul is tied even though it is negatively affecting or even destroying the important relationship in your life (husband, wife, kids, leaders and so on.

7. You have simultaneous experiences or moods as the person to whom your soul is tied. This can even include sickness, accidents, addictions, and so forth.

Do you know that he who Is joined to a harlot is one body with her? For the two "HE says" shall become one flesh

1 Corinthians 6:16

Soul Tie Nugget

Soul ties can also be relationships that are gifts from God. He uses them to help us to commit to one another. To stand firm and bring things through for completion. God wants us to be connected to one another so that we can live out his divine will for our lives.

CHAPTER TWO

SOUL TIE SIGNS AND SYMPTOMS

The idea behind the term soul mate is that there is one person created by God whom you are destined to spend your life with. Personally, I haven't read anything in the Bible about them and it is a distinctive way of thinking about relationships, but let's explore the different ways soul ties are created. Soul ties form in Godly ways and then they reveal how Satan twists and perverts them.

First, we have biological soul ties. These are created through our bloodline. We are tied to those who came before us and those who will come after us. We should have the strongest ties to our most immediate family members. Parent-child relationships are designed by God to last. **Genesis 1:28** states God has commissioned us to be fruitful and multiply. We are created as such helpless babies, completely dependent on the love, care, and attention of our parent. The desire to have children is so strongly implanted within us that Racheal Cries out in the Bible "Give me children, or else I will die, **Genesis 30:1**

So, we see that this is a strong God-given desire. God planned for us to be incredibly devoted to our families. Unfortunately, Satan has been busy from the beginning trying to destroy the importance of family ties. Satan is eager to attack the family unit and one of his earliest moves was to get siblings to be jealous of one another and ultimately commit the first murder. Soul ties aren't only about who you are connected to, it's also about how and why you're connected.

(ABORTION)

Consider how abortion plays into this. A woman rejects and murders her offspring prior to birth. But there is a connection between the two that is stronger than life and death. Therefore, so many women are overcome with depression, pain, and mourning after choosing to abort.

I can truly relate to this because I had an abortion around the age of 20. I was on a basketball scholarship at a junior college and when I became pregnant, I didn't know what to do or who I should even talk to. Back then you were almost considered a disgrace for getting pregnant and your family would disown you and you would be the talk of the town.

So, I was always very concerned about what people thought of me and remember I was in college on a basketball scholarship, so you know I didn't want anyone to find out. There was this girl on my team who had already had one and knew where to call and go for it. She gave me the information and I called, made the appointment, and went. I was so scared, but I felt like it was the only way. I didn't see no way of getting thru being pregnant even with the father saying it wasn't his. I felt like it was the only choice I had. So, as I'm in this room and all these different plugs and other equipment is around me, I was so scared but at the same time I was so ready to get this over with. All I could think about was getting rid of this secret and not allowing anyone to find out about it. So, I went thru the process and it was over physically but mentally, emotionally the problems had just begun. I became depressed and just miserable. My life changed for the worst and not the best. My soul was tied to an innocent baby that already had a heartbeat. I was so upset and miserable. I went thru life up and down and I totally lost my will to live. My soul was mourning the very part of It's being that was killed. That baby was a part of me, a part of my soul. I then started having suicidal thoughts and attempted to commit suicide at one point of my life because I was pregnant by my ex-husband and I lost it, I was so upset because I blamed myself for having the abortion. I felt like it was the cause of me losing my baby. I tried to commit suicide because my soul was longing to be connected to the baby I killed. So, until this day I blame myself because I feel if I hadn't had an abortion, I would have had all my babies I lost. I would have had 5 kids total. So, I'm still believing God to restore babies unto me so my soul will be at peace.

I told all of that to get to this part because after I severed the soul tie between me and my baby, I experienced these symptoms. I want to really let individuals know about soul ties and the importance of gaining knowledge and knowing the truth about them. Let me give you a few examples of different signs to look for that could affect you mentally and emotionally.

- **Increased suffering, daydreaming, struggle, or doubt**
- **Problems in your marriage**
- **Losing touch with your children**
- **Living more and more isolated or having a secret life**
- **Committing adultery or having abortions**
- **Experiencing mystical dreams or visions**

Those are just a few symptoms to look for when you feel you are still connected to an ungodly soul tie. Take heed and get the help you need to break free from being in bondage.

You are a spirit being in a body, with a mind will, and emotions. These three parts. The mind, the will, and emotions make up your human soul.

For what is a man profited, if he shall gain the whole, and lose his own soul? Or what shall a man give in exchange for his soul?

Deuteronomy 4: 29

CHAPTER THREE

SOUL MATES

What is a soul mate? A soul mate is a person with whom one has a feeling of deep or natural affinity. This may involve similarity, love, romance, platonic relationships, comfort, intimacy, sexuality, and sexual activity.

If you would ask yourself, have you ever felt like you had a soul mate? If so, take note of who and how was the relationship and did it bring happiness and peace? Soul mates come together to help remind each other of their purpose. They come together to help awaken each other and remind each other of who they really are. Sometimes soulmate relationships can blossom into forever, and other times they are too intense and need to be released. A positive soul tie only brings the best out of you, so take note of the actions of the people you choose to have in your life. Be mindful of negative and positive soul ties. I have an a few encounters with negative soul ties that brought misery and pain to my life. In addition, I had to fast and pray for God to release me from that relationship and grant me the freedom I desired. So, stay very aware of your relationships. Once you become entangled in a negative soul tie just know it's basically trying to take your soul. A positive soul tie will keep you in places where you can grow and prosper even as your soul prospers. We have all had an experience with a demonic force invading the heart and soul of someone we know, so we have to stay clear and pray for their soul and ask God to deliver them from the demonic spirit that is driving them to act the way they are acting. Prayer and fasting are very essential when you have realized you have become entangled in a soul tie.

  To me I see a soul mate as a good thing. I believe soul mates come together in order to make dreams and visions

CHAPTER FOUR
PARTS OF THE SOUL

There are three parts that make up your soul. The mind, the will, and the emotion. This clearly is proved by the Word of God. Proverbs 2:10 gives us the spiritual ground to prove that the mind is a part of the soul. This verse says "Wisdom will enter your heart and knowledge will be pleasant to your soul. In addition, **Psalms 139: 14** says, "My soul knows it well".

All parts of the soul have desires but desire in appetitive and spirited parts is not a matter of belief but about what is good and evil. The soul is what you are. The center of who you are. Your soul existed before you were born, and it will exist after you die. The Wikipedia states that the soul is the mental abilities of a living being: reason, character, feeling, consciousness, memory, perception, thinking, etc. A soul can be mortal or immortal.

Lamentations 3:20

My Soul remembers well. That indicates that the soul can remember things. So, by these things we can be clear that the mind as the organ to know, to consider, and to remember is a part of the soul.

Let's look at the second part of the soul and that is the will. To me the will is very broad. It is where you have numerous choices, whether good or evil. It is where you make decisions to live a life for Christ or you choose to live for someone else. So, your will is very broad it can become so entangled in many ways because there are so many opportunities this world brings. I chose to submit my will to God's and it's a continuing thing because I get distracted and get off course sometimes which causes a delay in my blessings and I then become confused and lost. When you say you believe in Christ you must know that you must submit your will to his will regardless of what you want and desire. In this walk there is two ways to go and that is to be in His perfect will or His permissive will. What is His perfect will?

Romans 12:2 says Do not be conformed to this present world, but be transformed by the renewing of your mind, so that you may test and approve what is the will of God – what is good and well-pleasing and perfect. The will of God is a plan for humanity. I can truly say I still struggle with God's will for my life because I have numerous gifts, very self-willed and I believe I can do anything I put my mind to, so I really fight with God over the will for my life. God has given me so many gifts I sometimes wonder why?? Yes, I said it I wonder how I use all these gifts and live in the carnal world where all they think about is education and money. I believe in faith and gifts, but I get lost in this canal minded environment I constantly am fighting to live in. So, I'm praying and seeking God for his will and then once I accept his perfect will all will be well.

Let's give insight on Permissive Will. So, what is a permissive will? The permissive will is not sinful but is not God's best for us. Be careful when you are choosing your mate, career, or just anything that gives life or is associated with your life. The permissive leaves a door open for extra problems and it eventually bites you back. How many times have you acknowledged God was giving you direction on a move in your life? He was telling you to go left and you chose to go right. How did that affect you? Did you run into unnecessary problems? I can answer those myself and say yes! So, we must decide which will we are going to follow. Sometimes you must ask God "What is it you want me to do" because we consistently tend to get off course. There is an article I found thru google called "What does God want me to do? It is written by; Patrick Oben. "God's will for us is general and specific. He will specifically instruct you regarding circumstances in your life, such as finances or relationships" **(Oben 2017)** These directions are truly specific to the individual and cannot be applied to someone else. You must learn to hear from God for yourself rather than trying to duplicate His guidance to another regarding their situation. I'm going to give you three core general things God wants us to do that Oben also said in his article.

1. God wants every one of us to be saved, through grace, by putting our faith in Jesus and when we do, we receive His spirit and come into a relationship with him.

2. God wants us to constantly fill our hearts with Word to continually grow in our relationship with him

3. God's will be for us to surrender the control of our lives to Him

These things are presented in a careful order, because each step makes way and empowers us for the next.

Truly my soul waiteth upon God from him cometh my salvation

Psalms 62:1

CHAPTER FIVE

TUG AND PULL SOUL TIE

Have you ever been connected to someone whether it was a boyfriend or girlfriend and you knew you were already tied to them but there was just something that would come and pull and tug on your spirit(soul) every once and a while, It presented itself as evil, heaviness, and just totally uncomfortable. I am a victim of being attached to a soul that's already destined to hell. I know it sounds crazy, but God uses the foolish to confound the wise. I know I would always feel this horrible feeling, deep in my soul that would make me so uncomfortable and I knew where it was coming from because I knew who I had tied my soul to. Two souls that aren't supposed to be together will always have confusion and misunderstandings. And believe it or not when the evil soul goes out and connects with another soul the other person can feel the cheating or disloyalty.

And we say we don't know when our mate is cheating, some don't but guess what most do. If you are being 100% committed just know a pure soul cannot lie. I finally chose to listen to my soul and take heed to the warning. The very thing you don't what to do is to be faithfully tied to someone and they are out sharing your soul with someone else. Lord have mercy. Just know whoever they sleep with attaches to your soul when they come back and sleep with you. So, the question you may be wondering is how do I break this soul tie? What do I need to do with my feelings, emotions, and most of all the love I have for this person? This was struggle for me because my whole life was engulfed in this man. He promised me I was his wife and his house was mine. I put so much time and energy in that promise that I lost my house, even though it went in foreclosure because the landlord wasn't paying the mortgage I didn't have enough energy to even fight because I was so torn and damaged emotionally I had no fight left for myself only for the so-called life he had promised me. He promised me so many things and I gravitated my life around his promises, that's what I call them. I was so far gone my soul had become in a horrible place because his intentions were never pure, and I had sold my soul to the devil. I had given up what God had called me to do to marry a man who never had any intentions on marrying me. He used me for sex even when I didn't want it, used me for my information because he wasn't from the U.S, used my sincerity for his purpose and left me out here to dry. I was so gone. He had my soul, mind and spirit. I was about to sacrifice my soul to this man only to be destroyed and eventually killed whether I killed myself or he killed me. I had lost my house, car, license, and I knew the devil was coming for my business and that was what I walked away with so that's what God wanted me to have and everything else that was taken was not even in his will for me. I can remember when I first moved to Atlanta in 2016 God told me to start your church and get you a building and just live in it, but I was so hard up for what wanted I totally ignored God and did what I wanted to do, and I am now suffering the consequences of my decisions. I am now working on doing fully what God has called me to do. I have given up trying to be a wife to a man who really doesn't want a wife and am now trying to focus on what I want as an individual and a person. We can be so caught up in what we want and forget who God has called us to be. I can truly say when I love, I love so hard I just put 150% in my relationship knowing my call and who God made me to be will suffer if I'm not getting that energy, I'm releasing out back.

See we as church folk has been taught that the enemy is always being sent on assignment. So, if God and the devil must have a discussion about us what makes us think we are not being put on assignment by God. God gave the devil permission to attack Job and it was about his faith and his soul. He made a decision and he said, "Thou He slay me, yet will I trust him" **Job 13:15**. So we have to make the same decision it doesn't matter what we lose in the process, how we feel in the process. What matter is if we give up on God. Where is our soul destined? Who did we choose? Did we give up on our faith? These are the questions that should be answered after the assignment is over because it will really allow you to see your strengths and weaknesses as a Believer in Christ. If we can go thru our assignment and find growth, then we know that it worked together for our good. Stop thinking that the devil has power, he only has a little and he can only use it by God's permission. Our whole lives were already predestined by God and even in the word it states; And I give unto them eternal life; and they shall never perish, neither shall any man pluck them out of my hand **(John 10:28)**

CHAPTER SIX

ENTANGLEMENT RELATIONSHIP

Are you in a relationship, or are you in an entanglement? A relationship is one in which both people are free to be themselves, yet there is no shortage of intimacy. No fear that doing what you love or being who you are or taking time for yourself will drive the other person away. In a relationship, neither person needs the other to "complete" them. Both people are awake to themselves, their feelings and thoughts, and are open to the flow of love and attention with one another.

Entanglements on the other hand feel very different.

SIGNS OF ENTANGLEMENT

1. **You keep having the same issues**
   -When you find yourself having the same old argument with your

partner for the umpteenth time, that's a pretty good sign you're likely in an entanglement.

2. You don't feel safe or understood

- One of the clearest signs of entanglement is that it is hard for one person to let the other person feel his or her feelings and tell the truth about them. Entanglements feel like you must shut down a part of yourself.

3. Someone always must be right

In a real relationship, each person is "awake" to his or her role in a problem, and the priority for both is relationship growth.

Those are just some examples of ways you could be in an entangled relationship. Just make sure you are aware of the possible ways that you could be hindered from being happy and being free.

I can truly say these were the same things going on in my relationship and we couldn't figure out what the problem was. We would pray together, fast and just do different things but in reality, the truth was we had been an entangled relationship for almost 3 years going around in circles not moving forward or growing. There were frustration and anger building because we couldn't figure out what was happening. So, my advice is to always self- evaluate yourself when you are in a relationship so you will know the truth and not be deceiving yourself.

CHAPTER 7

IMMATURE AND MATURE SOULS

What does it mean that the Soul is mature? If, you ask yourself the question "What do I expect from life? And you give an honest answer, the quality of that answer contains the response the question of the Soul's maturity (Wanderer 2015). If the immature Soul has spiritual objectives, then it may suspect that all important things take place in the Now, here and now, but the Soul still uses the present moment as a springboard to get to its future objectives. Immature souls' live lives based of their feelings and emotions while a mature soul know its ok to feel but it's how you deal with the feelings is what makes the difference. People often are taught that feelings are real in reality, they are because we do feel something behind every hurt and upset. When you become mature you begin to realize that if you deal with your feelings accordingly some problems you might run into may not affect you as it would if you dealt with them immaturely. A mature soul realizes life is a gift and it shouldn't be taken advantage of.

Never confuse a mature soul with an immature soul. I thought about this scripture while writing and it says "When I as a child I spoke like a child, I thought like a child, I reasoned like a child. When I became a man, I gave up childish ways.

1 Corinthians 13:11. This verse is very powerful to me especially writing on immature and mature souls. Many of us are so immature when it comes to Christ we want to be treated like babies and feel as if

no one should say anything to us. Well that why we have to get mature because God will use people to correct us and if we feel no one can correct us we will continue to live in sin and become entangled and our soul will become lost. It's time to grow up and become mature and reach the level God wants for you. Learn to listen and receive correction it is only to help your soul become prosperous.

CHAPTER EIGHT

SOUL FIGHT

Don't you realize, there is a fight going on. The flesh and the Spirit are in War. The Flesh wants to take over your mind, body, and soul. It wants to send you to hell. So, my advice to you is to have a made-up mind when it comes to where you want to spend eternity. So, the question is where? I chose long time ag I wanted to go to Heaven but my flesh sometimes gets the best of me and I am true enough to myself to say it sometimes win, but when I realize I'm heading in the wrong direction I began to fight and build my spirit man up so my flesh won't get the best of me. I would never tell you that it is easy, but I will say it's worth it. Do I still struggle with some things? Of course, I do I, but I don't allow them to take me out. You may ask, how do I fight? This battle is very hard. I would tell you to pray, fast, and stay in the Word (Bible). The Word is most powerful it is sharper than any two-edged sword so it will pierce your spirit and help you make better decisions. Always remember we have choices and we are not always going to make the right ones but just make sure you are fighting to instead of just allowing sin to control your mind and your actions. Life can be very tempting, but you always must put in the forefront of your mind that your soul has a place it must live one day. When you transition just know judgment day is waiting and God will judge you according to your unrighteousness and righteousness. What you do here on earth determines where your soul will live. I named this chapter Soul Fight because you need to know the importance of fighting while you are here on this earth. We aren't just here for any old reason; we are here to do the work of the Lord and to live according to His Word. To love others as He loves us and to just make our time on earth count for something other than just getting up every morning going to a 9 to 5. We have work to do down here and the more we work for the Kingdom the more strength we have to fight against the flesh. Your soul is in the biggest fight of its life. The only thing we can do as servants is to trust God and be obedient to Him and His Word. Never chose the world over Christ because the world is temporary, but God is forever. I would rather fight to live forever than to adhere to the standard of this wicked and crucial world. The world only promises heartaches and pains but with God you will experience those things, but HE promises to deliver us from them all.

CHAPTER NINE

DELIVER MY SOUL

He is my soul mate!

He is like a drug I am addicted to!

He will always have a piece of my heart!

These words follow one person who swept you off of your feet and mesmerized you like an intoxicating drug. You craved the time you spent with them and never got enough. The word affectionately refers to these people as our soulmates, someone our hearts will always be joined to regardless of time or place. It's a relationship, even after all these years, that you use to measure others. It almost sounds romantic doesn't it? It is not a soul mate but an ungodly emotional soul tie that allows demons of sadness and loss to torment you. Soul ties are established either through sexual sin or emotional control and manipulation. So, you will eventually have to make a choice. You will have to continue to actively confess and repent for what you allowed. Do you have a person like this in your life that has taken up way too much of your thoughts? Are you ready to return that part of your heart to God so peace can reside where sadness dwells?

3 Steps to Break – Up with an Ungodly Soul Tie

1. Confess and repent for idolatry that allowed this person a place above God in your heart by speaking out loud: " I confess and repent for allowing (NAME) to become an idol in my life and I cancel every demonic assignment of idolatry in the name and blood of Jesus Christ.

2. Break all word curses spoken over your heart by repeating" I break every word curse I have spoken over my heart and soul regarding (NAME) in the name and blood of Jesus Christ. I now declare them null and void."

3. Break the ungodly soul tie by speaking out loud; " I now break and

sever the ungodly soul tie between (NAME) and myself, and myself and (NAME) in the name and blood of Jesus Christ and declare that every spirit of disappointment, sadness, and loss associated with the soul tie must go in the name of JESUS CHRIST".

Always remember the enemy will find ways to attack you so just stay prayed up and acknowledge your weaknesses and know God is forever with you.

Notes and Scripture Reference

_____

_____

_____

_____

_____

_____

_____

What are some ways you have identified you may be in a soul tie?

_____

_____

_____

_____

_____

_____

Name the people or person

_____

_____

_____

_____

_____

_____

_____

How do you think the soul tie came about?

_____

_____

_____

_____

_____

_____

_____

_____

QUALITY OVER QUANTITY

How many times have you chose quantity over quality? I can recall many times of choosing something or someone that had more. As I became older and wiser, I realized quantity didn't matter if abuse, neglect, mistreatment, and etc. was involved in it. I just couldn't see that from the beginning because I was always taught make sure you find a man that has money and that can take care of you but nobody ever told me to make sure they treat you with proper care. I always wondered why I always ended up with a man who would mistreat me and know I see why. God clearly spoke to me one day in that area of my life, but I then also included it to all the areas of my life because it was some powerful wisdom. I am now able to se the truth about anything when it comes to my life. This is just some extra wisdom you can use and apply to your life. Stop looking for

how much and start looking at how you are treated.

THE SOUL

The Soul is the most important part of the body. The ending results is Heaven or Hell.

What kind of Life would you choose? A life of sin and fun or a life of peace and obedience.

Who chooses life and then abandons their peace. Who chooses peace then abandons their life.

Questions are so important when it comes to recognizing changes that needs to be made in your life.

Ask yourself! Give room to your mind and problems so you can be able to have a clear view of everything going on around you.

If not, danger will continue to lurk until it finds a resting place in your life. Your soul and mind longs for peace but at the end of life it longs for a resting place.

WHICH WILL YOU CHOOSE?

For Bookings: Speaking and more

Dr. Shameka Pointer

Open Heart Counseling Services, Inc.

149 S. McDonough St Ste 260

Jonesboro, Ga 30236

770-905-2517

FACEBOOK

DrSHAMEKA POINTER

INSTAGRAM

Dr. Shameka R. Pointer, CpsyD.

Made in the USA
Columbia, SC
17 May 2024